BECOMING INTERNATIONAL

WORKING AND WRITING FOR CHANGE
Series Editors: Steve Parks and Jessica Pauszek

The Writing and Working for Change series began during the 100th anniversary celebrations of NCTE. It was designed to recognize the collective work of teachers of English, Writing, Composition, and Rhetoric to work within and across diverse identities to ensure the field recognize and respect language, educational, political, and social rights of all students, teachers, and community members. While initially solely focused on the work of NCTE/CCCC Special Interest Groups and Caucuses, the series now includes texts written by individuals in partnership with other communities struggling for social recognition and justice.

Books in the Series

CCCC/NCTE Caucuses

History of the Black Caucus National Council Teachers of English by Marianna White Davis

Listening to Our Elders: Working and Writing for Social Change by Samantha Blackmon, Cristina Kirklighter, and Steve Parks

Building a Community, Having a Home: A History of the Conference on College Composition and Communication edited by Jennifer Sano-Franchini, Terese Guinsatao Monberg, K. Hyoejin Yoon

Community Publications

Becoming International: Musings on Studying Abroad in America, edited by Sadie Shorr-Parks

Dreams and Nightmares: I Fled Alone to the United States When I Was Fourteen by Liliana Velásquez. Edited and translated by Mark Lyon

The Weight of My Armor: Creative Nonfiction and Poetry by the Syracuse Veterans' Writing Group, edited by Ivy Kleinbart, Peter McShane, and Eileen Schell

PHD to PhD: How Education Saved My Life by Elaine Richardson

BECOMING INTERNATIONAL

Musings on Studying Abroad in America

Editor: Sadie Shorr-Parks
Associate Editor: Deborah J. McGraw

Parlor Press
Anderson, South Carolina
www.parlorpress.com

Parlor Press LLC, Anderson, South Carolina, USA

Printed in the United States of America on acid-free paper.

Library of Congress Cataloging-in-Publication Data on File

1 2 3 4 5

978-1-64317-034-3 (paperback)
978-1-64317-035-0 (PDF)
978-1-64317-036-7 (ePub)

WORKING AND WRITING FOR CHANGE
An Imprint Series of Parlor Press
Series Editors: Steve Parks and Jessica Pauszek

Editor: Sadie Shorr-Parks, Shepherd University
Associate Editor: Deborah McGraw, Syracuse University
Designer: Elizabeth Parks, elizabethannparks@gmail.com

Parlor Press, LLC is an independent publisher of scholarly and trade titles
in print and multimedia formats. This book is available in paper and eBook
formats from Parlor Press on the World Wide Web at http://www.parlor-
press.com or through online and brick-and-mortar bookstores. For submis-
sion information or to find out about Parlor Press publications, write to Parlor Press, 3015 Brackenberry Drive, Anderson, South Carolina, 29621, or
email editor@parlorpress.com.

Contents

Acknowledgments

Hooray to the universe for getting New City Community Press Founder and Director, Steve Parks, and English Language Institute director, David Lind, together for coffee on a 2017 Madrileño summer day!

With gratitude to David Lind for his vision to do a project that reaped many unexpected gifts and for his enthusiasm.

In appreciation to the Dean of University College, Michael Frasciello, for his support throughout the life of the project.

A special thanks also to my fellow English Language Institute teachers Jessica Cimino Schmidt, Deb Diemont, Mary Lou Haroian, Janna Kholeva, Becky Mindek, Olga Oganesyan, Jackie Schneider-Revette, and Connie Walters whose students' work is published here. The teachers' care and dedication enabled the students to articulate ideas in their own voice.

Thank you to the English Language Institute at Syracuse University student services staff, Danielle Benjamin and Jackie Monsour, for all of their behind-the-scenes work.

Finally, applause for the 2017-2018 academic year English Language Institute students for their willingness to take a leap of faith in a language not their own. The pieces in this book are deeply important to them. These stories and poems represent who these accidental authors were, who they are, and who they will become.

—Amy Walker, English Language Institute at Syracuse University

Photo Credits

Page 4: "Multilingual road sign in Glendale, CA" by Eli Carrico (Flickr user: ShapeThings)

Page 10: "Arad, Israel Multilingual sign bookstore" by J Brew (Flickr user: brewbooks)

Page 16: "Travel notebook page, 14.-16.6.2012" by Lauramandelbaum

Page 18: "Multilingual bus station sign in Erenhot" by Terfili

Page 25: "'Rows', Carl Plate, collage 1975" by Alleyane Catherine Plate

Page 30: "Mezzanine at the exit C of Xibeiwang Station" by N509FZ

Page 32: "Camera-Stencil-Graffiti" by Andreas Schwarzkopf

Page 36: "Old-fashioned telephone sign" by pelican

Page 38: "Algarve 2014 (9)" by Benoît Prieur - CC-BY-SA

Page 45: "Stencil (183415001)" by Luis Rodriguez Ochoa

All of the these photos are used under the Creative Commons Attribution license. For more about this license, please visit
https://creativecommons.org/licenses/by/2.0/

Introduction

Are you currently studying abroad in the United States or contemplating doing so? Well, imagine having a companion while abroad. Imagine you could learn what is truly on another international student's mind and have words to comfort you as you adapt to a new culture and academic environment.

Becoming International: Musings on Studying Abroad in America can be your companion.

This book is the culmination of a 2017–2018 academic year project at Syracuse University's English Language Institute (ELI). For this project, these ELI students responded to a variety of writing prompts from New City Community Press. Many did not think of themselves as authors. At first many did not see the benefit of autobiographical or creative writing because their sole reason for attending the ELI was to obtain enough English proficiency for admission to an American undergraduate or graduate degree program. Since they were facing such high stakes, some questioned how participating in this project would contribute to their goal.

However, once the project was underway, unexpected positive outcomes started to appear for both the ELI students and their teachers. We were all in these wonderful "workshop bubbles." In many respects, this project felt like a collaboration between peers rather than between teachers and students. Each participant contributed their strengths. Each participant was willing to grow in new ways.

The authors were brave. They allowed themselves to be vulnerable. They wrote about personal topics in a language that they had varying degrees of control over. As they drafted pieces in response to the New City Community Press prompts and discussed the ideas in those drafts, autobiographical details surfaced of which they had previously been unaware.

Throughout the process, the writers had a surprising level of determination to accurately express their ideas in English. They took themselves seriously.

The students and teachers felt joy when they realized something special was happening. The students were gaining more confidence in their English and becoming more grounded in this U.S. collegiate environment. As a teacher, it was very gratifying to witness this unfolding.

If you are currently studying abroad or contemplating doing so, you may want to reflect on the following questions as you read *Becoming International: Musing on Studying Abroad in America*. You may also benefit from answering these questions and comparing your responses to the writers' responses. Answering these questions will make you more self-aware and enable you to be more proactive. Your answers might act as anchors in your life. If you are grounded, your chances of being successful on an American academic campus are higher.

- What is the meaning of home to you?
- What are important memories that can give you strength while abroad?
- Look around you. Which stranger or acquaintance might become a source of assistance?
- What are some ways that you can learn to be independent?
- How can you manage or overcome doubts regarding your decision to study abroad?
- If you could acquire some special skills that would help you to succeed while studying in the United States, what would they be?

Amy M. Walker
Instructional Language Coordinator
English Language Institute
Syracuse University

MIRAR
LOOK
ԱՆԱ

WHAT A JOURNAL DOES

Yuto Sean Nakao

This is my journal. It makes me remember clearly what I did because that is what a journal does. I got it a week before I left Japan. I started journaling the day before I left.

There are a couple of reasons I began journaling. One of them is improving my English. On the first page, the grammar is awful. Even though I'm still not good at grammar, I was even worse at the beginning. This means I can see my progress.

I also journal because I don't want to forget my memories of Syracuse. It reminds of my daily life there. Time goes by. People forget. I think it's really important to keep something that reminds you of your precious memories, such as a picture or a journal.

It will be one of your treasures ten to twenty years later.

IN MY HOME
Yuan Cheng

Home is a place where I can stay with my mom. Mom is the most important person in my life. She always makes me feel warm and comfortable. I can tell my mom all my secrets in our home. Mom will cook a lot of delicious food for me, like Sichuan food, which is very spicy and always makes me miss home. Sometimes I don't have to bring keys with me because mom will help me open the door. I can feel free to eat, sleep, and take a shower at home. I also can invite my friends to come to my home.

I have a cat in my home, and his name is Pipi. He always stays at home because he is afraid of outside. When I see a cat, I will think about Pipi. In my home there are goldfish, and my cat always sits in front of the goldfish. Pipi sometimes try to catch the goldfish and eat them.

Pipi always makes me miss my home.

I plant a lot of flowers and vegetables in my yard, such as roses, tomatoes, oranges, and strawberries. My mom often forgets to give the plants some water, so I have to remind my mom many times. I think my mom has a special smell. Home is a private place that strange people cannot enter. Home makes me feel safe.

HOME ALWAYS WAITS FOR ME

Ai Guan

Home always waits for me, even when I go to faraway places or leave for a long time, so I never feel lonely. Home has deeper meaning than just 'a building.' It is where the heart is. Home brings me different kinds of emotion.

I love my home because of my family. They help me a lot, not only in my studies but also in my life. When I encounter some problems, they always try their best to ease my mind and teach how to avoid these problems. Sometimes when I have a conflict with others, they patiently tell me the best way to solve it. They prefer to educate me, which is the most impressive part. Therefore, I learned a lot from my family, who were my first teachers.

Furthermore, home is my most pleasurable place. I do not need to worry too much. On the weekend, we talk to each other, play with my little sister, and enjoy some activities. Since I have my home, I feel warm, and so I want to give other people warmth, too. Therefore, I am really thankful for my whole family.

When the different festivals are coming, we stay together at home and cook great meals. For example, Spring Festival is a significant day for Chinese people. To celebrate, we always buy lots of meat and vegetables, and then we cook. At midnight, we make dumplings and watch TV shows together. This meal is called "family reunion meal." My home makes me feel safe and joyful.

For me, home is the symbol of love. My parents, my sister, and I established a home. I'm lucky to have it.

KITTEN GAMES
Yicheng Tie

Home, sweet home. Home means a place full of laughter and happiness, a place full of love and peace. Moreover, home is where I stay with my family and my kittens. Every time I go back to my home, my mom always cooks for my family. (She really has a wonderful talent in cooking.) My dad is never at home since he works all the time. And my little kittens, they just play their own kitten games. Turning, fighting, jumping and meow-meow. After they see me, they push me over and give me a kitten hug. (I mean, they walk around me and try to jump on me.) And then, my mom comes out from the kitchen and smiles at me, "Welcome back, feel hungry? Clean your hands, and let's have a lunch." The weather is great. The sunlight is beautiful, and everything my mom cooked has a magic taste. Its name is "Mom's homemade dishes." While we're eating, my little kittens always sit on my legs. They are really full of curiosity and want to taste what I'm eating. Maybe it's because everything my mom cooks is very delicious. Every time they try to eat human food, my mom will scream at them, like, "Don't eat that! Don't stay at Huhu's (my nickname) legs! You naughty little kittens!" After lunch, when I want to have a nap, my cats always sleep with me. The smell of laundry detergent on the sheets and the smell of cats wash around me. The sun makes me feel warm. Every time I feel this, I know I'm at home. I stay with people and cats that I love. They make me feel peace and love, safety and happiness.

MY GRANDMOTHER'S HOUSE

Anonymous

My grandmother's house is located in Dammam, which is in the eastern province of Saudi Arabia. It was built in 2006. Her house is on the corner of the street. It is white with red bricks on the top, and it has two floors. In addition, there are rooms for me, my siblings, and my uncle's family on the second floor. My grandmother's house is near to the Arabian Gulf and the Bahrain. There are many restaurants and supermarkets in the same district.

This place was very important to me before my grandmother passed away last year. I loved being there for many reasons. First, I made a lot of memories there, especially with my grandmother. I spent most of my vacations with her, and we usually travelled together. Second, most of our special occasions took place in her house. My relatives always came there for celebrating. Third, every time I came there she cooked my favorite kinds of food, even if she was tired or sick. At the same time, I acquired more knowledge by learning from my grandmother's life and her advice. All in all, I believe that what makes a place important and special for you is the person who lives there.

I KNOW EVERY ROCK IN THE OCEAN

Joakim Maaseidvaag Olsen

There are many hidden pearls in Norway, but one of the most rustic ones is Risor. The town of Risor is located in southern Norway, and it has a beautiful view of the open ocean, Skagerrak. Skagerrak, which is the ocean dividing Denmark and Norway, gives a view out over an unforgiving scenery: the cliffs, boat life, and one beautiful lighthouse. Further on, the rustic feeling comes within the city walls. This is where the old houses from the early 1900's are located. The charm these houses give, with thick wooden planks which was a common style of building houses in the period, is unforgettable. The landscape around Risor surrounds the little town with high cliffs and hiking opportunities. The most popular activity for visitors is to take a hike up the cliff and look at the old World War II museum. The museum is operated by people who have ties back to World War II. The bunkers used in World War II are also located on top of the cliff. To sum up, if you are planning on a trip to Norway, Risor is the place to visit.

Risor also ties me to family because my dad is from Risor and my grandmother has lived there her entire life. At a young age, this was the place I learned to swim with my dad's proud face watching over me. It didn't always go that well, so he had to be ready to fish me up if he saw me struggling. I also had my first fishing experience here. Dad and I took a hike to a nice location that his dad had shown him when my dad was younger. In fact, this turned out to be the best spot in Risor to catch some fish. We had a whole bucket full of fish heading home. Also, a boating experience in Risor is something that has stuck to my memory. My father taught me how to drive a boat at the age of thirteen. As a result, with good grandparents and a sponsored boat for me and my sister, I am used to endless hours on the ocean and comfortable enough to say that I know every little rock in the ocean outside our house in Risor. To sum up, the ties I have to this place give me happiness, joy, and pictures, which will last a lifetime.

A HOLY PLACE FOR MY LIFE

Zhi Li

Daocheng is located in the Sichuan Province, which is in southern China. It has been attracting thousands of Chinese and foreign travelers due to its breathtaking natural scenery. The area of Daocheng is located on an average elevation of 3,800 meters. There are many endangered species living in Daocheng. For example, Daocheng has golden monkeys, water deer, and so on. Jambeyang mountain, Chana Dorje Mountain, and Chenrezig Mountain are the three main mountains, and they are considered some of the most holy places in China.

I have been attracted to Daocheng since three years ago when I saw a blogger posted some amazing and beautiful photos of Daocheng. The limpid lake water and magnificent mountain leaped to my eyes, and I imagined that I could breathe fresh air from the soul on the ground. I promised that I would go to Daocheng in the future to have a wonderful vacation. Another reason Daocheng is special for me is because it is the place I was born, although I have not been there since that time. It's very lucky to have such a beautiful holy place in my hometown, and it's worth it for me to have a look. I am looking forward to traveling to Daocheng with someone very important to me.

THE SKY CAN BE THE RIVER

Yinqi Chang

Today I want to introduce a very incredible landscape in our country called "The Mirror of the Sky." It is located in Qinghai Province in China. It is a salty lake called "Cha ka." It is transparent because it is so full of salt. It is a fresh lake. The depth of the lake is really low, so people can wander across this lake. It is called "The Mirror of the Sky" because the water is clear enough to reflect the scene of the sky. When people turn over this picture, the sky can be the river. Also, the river can be the sky. If there are some people walking on the river, their inverted image can also change into their real body. It is really amazing.

I really like these images in two different ways. First, although the color of this picture is really simple, it gives me a visual impact. I have an intensive feeling that I want to go to this lake as soon as possible. Then, I can take this kind of picture by myself. In addition, this picture gives me a feeling of silence. Few people walk on this lake, and the sky is really clear. If I walk on the lake and enjoy the landscape with my heart, I will forget everything and take myself into the nature. That is why I think "Cha ka" River is worth visiting.

THE BELL TOWER

Chuanjie Jian

The Bell Tower is located in center of the Xi'an and was built in 1384 during the early Ming Dynasty. The Bell Tower is thirty-six meters high, and it covers an area of 1377 square meters. There is a large bell on the tower, and the bell was used to wake up citizens every day. Now the Bell Tower has become symbol of Xi'an. It represents the intelligence of ancient people.

When I look at the tower, I feel that I can see my hometown and many memories emerge in my mind. The Bell Tower is just thirty-six meters high, so people probably cannot see it in other cities. However, the Bell Tower can be seen everywhere in Xi'an because the Xi'an government formulated a regulation. Every edifice which surrounds the Bell Tower cannot surpass the height of the Bell Tower, so people can see the Bell Tower from far away. Besides, when I went to my high school with my best friends, we always needed to pass the Bell Tower. We lived in the same neighborhood. When I remember the Bell Tower, I think of my best friend, although we cannot see each other now. Finally, there are many malls around the area. I often take the metro and get off at the Bell Tower station with my mother and friends. I can think of wonderful times when I look at this picture.

LOVELY SUMMER

Haochen Feng

Everyone must have a picture with special meaning. I have a picture that was taken in the summer of 2015. The location of this picture is northern China. It shows a couple's back, which is me and my boyfriend, Allen. We were traveling to the city nearby his hometown by car with his family and his best friends.

It was the second year we had been together. Allen had just graduated from high school. It was not easy for us in those two years, since both of us are young and our minds were not mature yet. It was the first time I met his whole family. His family was really friendly to me. They took me to eat lots of delicious food that I had never tried before. His friends are friendly and amicable. We watched a movie together, shared jokes, and talked about the future with each other. At the same time, we celebrated Allen's nineteenth birthday. We had a lovely dinner together, and we went to bathe in a hot spring, which is so wonderful that it could help you relax your mind and body. I miss that summer so much. I can say that was the one of the best summers of my life.

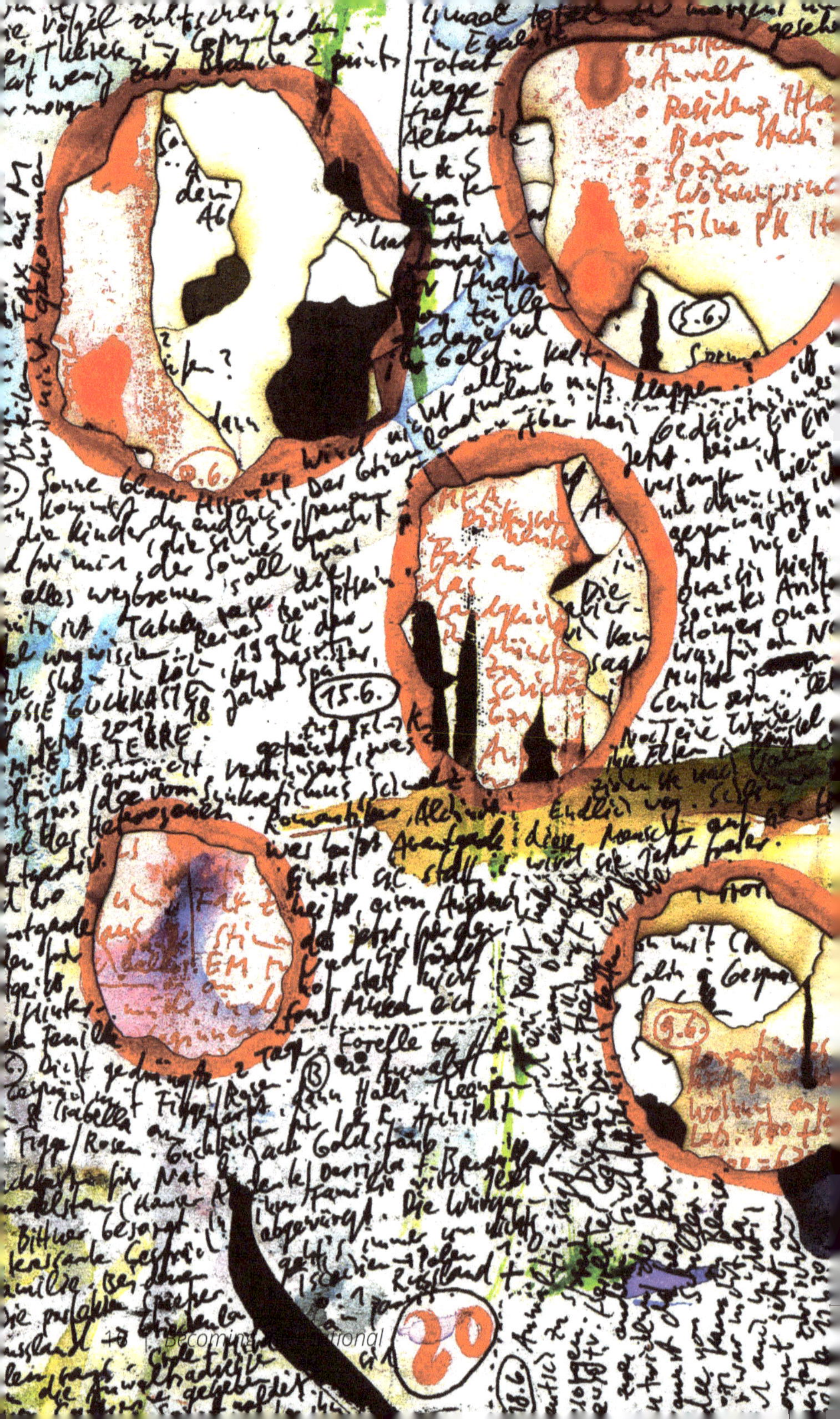
15.6.
9.6.
5.6.
20

A SEED

Dingyuan Wei

"If you really want to study movies in American, just do it." After my mother said that to me, I decided to come to the United States. "Study in America," it was like a seed that was planted in my mind. I had this seed since I was fourteen-years-old, but I did not have an opportunity to make it start to grow. When I got my grades in Arts, I knew that I didn't stand a chance to go to my dream school. I felt like I was a loser, and I lost myself. But one day the seed brought a light into my dark life when I discussed my thoughts with my mother. After that, we decided to make the seed grow. I began to study for the TOEFL. I consulted with my friends who are studying in America, and with their help, I finally got the offer from ELI at Syracuse University. After I got my plane ticket to Syracuse, I packed my bag and waited for the flight date to come. I really appreciate that my mother helped me make the decision to go to America, and I am glad to have the chance to keep nurturing my seed.

前门上车 后门下车 无人售票 票价一元
不设找零 主动投币 月票请出示

夏季　首班：06：30　末班：19：30　　冬季　首班：06：30　末班：18：30

1 公路口岸　铁蒙大药房 → 安泰木业

公路口岸　利丰汽车城　市医院　税务分局　蒙奥国际家具建材城（东门）　税务局　金茂建材　长途汽车站　铁路小区　海天小区　东统建材　铁蒙大药房　东城派出所　金叶时代广场　华联商厦　惠丰商贸城东门　义乌商贸南门　蒙古酒吧　第二小学　三星建材城　龙推国际建材城　爱民花园　液化气公司　海天水泥　蒙奥加油站　第六加油站　工业园区

BUS

ХИЛИЙН БООМТ
ЛИ ФЭН МАШИН ТЭРЭГНИЙ ХОТ
ХОТЫН ЭМНЭЛЭГ
ТАТВАРЫН САЛБАР ТОВЧОО
ШЭН ТҮН ОЛОН УЛСЫН ЗАХЫН ЗҮҮН ХААЛГА
ТАТВАРЫН ТОВЧОО
ЖИН МАО БАРИЛГЫН МАТЭРИАЛ
АВТО ВОКЗАЛ
ТОМОР ЗАМЫН АЖИЛЧИНЫ БАЙР
ГААЛИЙН АЖИЛЧИНЫ БАЙР
ЗҮҮН НИЙТИЙН БАЙР
ТИЕ МЭН АПТЕК
ЗҮҮН ХОТ ДҮҮРГИЙН ЦАГДААГИЙН ХЭСЭГ
ЖИН Е ХУДАЛДААНЫ ТАЛБАЙ
ХУА ЛИАНЬ ХУДАЛДААНЫ ТАЛБАЙ

ВЭН ЖЭУ ЗАХЫН ЗҮҮН ХААЛГА
И Ү ЗАХЫН ӨМНӨ ХААЛГА
МОНГОЛ БААР
ХОЁРДУГААР БАГА СУРГУУЛЬ
САН ШИН БАРИЛГЫН МАТЭРИАЛЫН ЗА
ЛУН ШИАН БАРИЛГЫН МАТЭРИАЛЫН З.
АЙ МИН ЛИН ЦЭЦЭРЛЭГ
ГАЗ ШИНГЭРҮҮЛТИЙН КОМПАНИ
ХАЙ ЛУН ЗАСВАРЫН ГАЗАР
МЭН ГАО ЦЕМЕНТ
ЗУРГААДУГААР ШАТАХУУН КОЛО
АЖ ҮЙЛДВЭРИЙН ХОРООЛ
НӨХӨРЛӨЛ МОДОН ХЭРЭГСЭЛ
АН ТАЙ МОДОН ХЭРЭГСЭЛ

WHEN I HAD TO LEAVE MY HOMETOWN

Tianyu Ye

One week before I had to leave my hometown, I felt stressed, nervous, and busy. Even though I wasn't yet leaving my parents, I already missed them. I also prepared lots of supplies such as, Lao Gan Ma, duck neck, and tea. All of those snacks are traditional Chinese snacks. I thought carefully about what I should prepare. I hung out with my friends because I would miss them so much. I said goodbye to my grandparents, and then I had to go to the airport and then to the United States.

SOFT PAJAMAS
Yan Zhu

The day I left my hometown, I wore my soft pajamas to the airport. I was not aware if other people were looking at me or not. When I sat on the plane, I put on my blindfold and cozy slippers. After that, I started sleeping. I only woke up when the airline stewardesses provided food. The last time I woke up, the plane had already landed at Kennedy International Airport. During that journey, I just felt numb.

THIS WOMAN WAS REALLY KIND

Yingqi Chang

When I got on the plane, I felt sleepy. As a result, I slept during the whole journey. When I woke up, the flight attendant said that because of a delay, my plane to Syracuse had already taken off. At that point, I felt scared. This was my first time to face such a situation. I really felt nervous because my English was not good at that time.

A passenger who sat close to me recognized that I really felt frightened. She asked me why I felt so nervous. I said it was because this was my first flight to the U.S. alone. I did not know how to solve this problem. The woman was really kind. She told me the specific procedure to handle this situation. I really appreciated her help. After I got off the plane, I followed her instructions, which told me how to get the connecting flight.

With the help of the crewmember, I then filled out the boarding form and got a one-day visa in Canada. In addition, the airport booked a hotel for us to live in. When I entered the room, I felt really relaxed. The room was really spacious. It was really functional and tidy. I connected the Wi-Fi and got on Facetime with my family members. Then I got a shower and slept well. The next morning the hotel's bus took us to the airport. In the end, we arrived at Syracuse successfully. To sum up, the experience was really impressive. I will never forget it.

AN EMBARRASSING EXPERIENCE IN THE U.S.

Yang Zhang

Does anyone know what this is?

Before I start my presentation, I want to ask you a question. Have you ever lost your baggage in the airport? Unfortunately, this happened to me the first day I landed.

A picture came from the person who took my baggage at the baggage claim. I found it by myself, and I almost thought that it was mine because it really looks the same as my baggage. When I became aware that my baggage was lost, I was worried about it. I was scared that it couldn't be found. My clothes, my shoes, and my other things were all in that case. At this time, I felt angry with that person who took my baggage to her house.

When I told the baggage helper about my problem, it was so embarrassing. On the one hand, my speaking is not good for communication. On the other hand, I felt worried, so I couldn't speak clearly about my problem. The baggage helper comforted me and began patient questioning. I said to him, "Maybe someone took the wrong baggage?" Then he gave me this ticket and asked me some questions. Then he said they needed some time to find it, and maybe three days later they would contact me.

WRITER OF LIFE
Dingyuan Wei

"Welcome to United Airlines."

I thought, *finally, I can go to America!* I took off my coat then looked at my new tattoo "carpe diem" that I had just gotten to commemorate my decision to study in America. I tried to be more excited and happy. While on this flight, I asked myself, *how do I feel about the fact that I am finally going to America? What do I think about the future?* However, as I tried to answer these questions, I didn't feel excited at all. I just felt sleepy and hungry. The day was becoming a normal flight day. I fell asleep for the whole flight.

When I transferred to another flight to Syracuse, I tried to figure out the reason why I didn't feel any excitement. As I thought, I would answer, *maybe I was imagining too much about this travel before*. Too much expectation would ruin the reality that life will give me various surprises. I don't need to try to be a writer of life. I just need to savor the moment and enjoy the surprises in my future. In this way, I can gain more excitement than I expected.

THE UPPER WIND

Haihang Yang

I felt excited to go to college in the US, and I couldn't wait. After I checked all my stuff and got the ticket, my family and I just sat near the entrance. The process of waiting annoyed me. When I checked the clock, it was time to go. I said, "Don't follow me" to my parents. As soon as I walked in the entrance, I started to cry. I turned around and found my parents were crying, too. At this time, I swore I didn't want to go abroad anymore. I regretted not staying with my parents for more time.

When I walked on to the airplane, I figured out that everybody has to go abroad to study. I put my bag above my seat and just sat. There was a girl who sat next to me. She seemed to be an eight-year-old child, and she didn't want to talk to me. When the plane took off, I felt a little bit sleepy. After a while, a baby started crying. It bothered me a lot, and I hated that. I couldn't even sleep. However, the stewardess soon came out with the dining car, and I was so happy. I was starved, and, finally, the baby didn't cry for a while. I could sleep for a while and no one could bother me. I woke up when the upper wind was so heavy. The baby, everything that I have been through, is all new. Finally, the plane touched down and the new life began.

SPEAK WELL AND MAKE FRIENDS

Anonymous

When I left my country by plane, my mind was very complex. I thought three things. Let me show you what I thought on the plane. First, I thought, *what's the American view*. Before I had never been to America, so I was really looking forward to arriving in America. I thought a lot until I fell to sleep, fell into my dream. Second, I thought about my parents. I missed them very much. I hoped they didn't worry about me. When I woke up on the plane, I was crying due to missing my parents. I hoped they could take care of themselves. Finally, I thought about studying English. I didn't know how I could adapt to American life in an all English country. I would need to work hard to study English, adapt to the English language, to speak well, and make friends. I hoped I could learn English well and make friends using English.

I thought all about my future in America, I was looking forward to learning in America.

THE HEADACHES

Zhichao Xue

I always got headaches when on a plane. I couldn't eat anything because of my headaches. I couldn't watch anything anymore because of the headaches. I couldn't get any sleep because of the headaches. I was suffering from traveling alone. This is my mind. When is this going to be over!

THE STORY OF LOVE

Jing Di, Xiangyi Wang, & "Viki"

Life is confusing in a new city
Perplexed
Out of parental control
Overly enthusiastic
A charming city to live
Positive
Miss family and hometown
Lonely
Walk in the falling snow
Cozy
Falling in love in Syracuse

NEW YORK CITY: SUNSHINE AND DARKNESS

Yoojeong Seo, Yangzhi Xiao, & Tianqi Yao

Yellow cabs, high-rise,
Desiring eyes, seeking dreams.
From the Far East, carrying dreams to America.
It's as though every shining light welcomes you,
But the lights are just shining for themselves.
New York, you lift me up,
But you throw me down even harder.
Roam around the little paths,
Luxury and romance,
Lingering in the sunset,
Life passes like a dream.
Desirable city, dazzled by hearts.
Money, reputation, lust.
Don't you forget who you are.
Don't hesitate. Straight forward. Keep moving

HELLO 后厂村

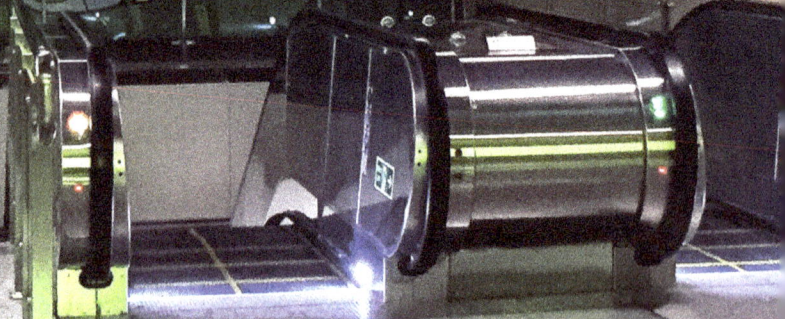

WHAT GOES UP
Yoojeong Seo

The line "New York, you lift me up" contains not only a positive meaning but also a negative meaning. If someone's position in life goes up, or if physically someone climbs up high, it is easy to fall down. Thus, this line explains that New York can make one's dream come true and bring them happiness. However, in another way, it will be easy to lose everything, like their dream, money, and happiness. Thus, going up is not always a good thing. When people enjoy their lives, they should be careful about falling down at the same time.

AN UNFORGETTABLE PHOTO

Young Yang

My girlfriend and I had a common dream, though she wanted to go abroad to school and pursue our life together. We had been in love for six years. We couldn't find desirable jobs to support our daily life expenditures. To be honest, it was very difficult for us to make the decision that we were going to go study abroad at Syracuse University. However, we couldn't get our marriage certificate in China because of a shortage of time. This was a very sad situation for us to experience before we arrived in the USA. She wanted me to do as much as I could to remedy it.

One day after we had been in the USA for several days, my uncle drove us around Washington DC. For me, it was an extremely important and unforgettable day in my life. On that day, when we were walking down the line of the Washington Monument is when I stopped walking and took out the ring. I asked Jenny to marry me and put the ring on her finger. I knew the camera was going to catch this moment, and I will save this picture forever. I never thought I would propose to Jenny in another country that is so far from our country. Now I think it might be destiny between me and Jenny that leads us to be together on our way to the future.

MY BOOTS
Yang Zhang

I remember when I saw the email suggesting I buy winter wear at Walmart, I couldn't understand this. I thought, why do we have to buy winter items? I already had enough warm winter clothes because Korean winters are also very cold.

Last year when I came to Syracuse, it showed right away why we needed more winter items. When I came here, Syracuse's weather was so, so, so cold. There was also a very snowy week where the temperature was -20 degrees Celsius. Korean winters can be snowy, but we didn't have as much snow as Syracuse. When it was a snowy day in Korea, it was enough if I wore thick socks and sneakers. So, when I arrived in Syracuse, I had only sneakers. But the roads in Syracuse were coldest then, and every time I walked my feet were getting very cold. So, I went to buy snow boots on the first weekend there. They are very thick and warm. I will never get wet again, and my boots help me to adapt to my new surroundings and weather.

I realized that Syracuse is really a snowy city, like Frozen. The snow amazed me, so I took pictures of the trees and roads, the cars and the houses. Now when it's snowy, I always wear my boots, and I have realized the importance of snow boots. I'm getting more and more familiar with Syracuse now, but still I hope spring comes in a hurry

BECOMING INDEPENDENT

Yongbin Yang

I'm eighteen-years-old. I'm not living with my parents right now. This is really influencing my life. In China, most children rely on their parents until they go to university. Parents always handle all the issues the child needs to care about, like their grades in school. Even on weekends parents could find another class, but they don't care about the child's feelings. They don't want their child to lose. Unfortunately, I'm one of those children. I lived with my parents, and during that time I relied on my parents during difficult situations, never thinking about the consequences of what I did. In my mind, my parents should handle all of it.

However, I have been totally different since I came here. In the United States, the children are extremely different from the children in China. I went to the United States three years ago to attend Simon Camp with my friends. I had five days of native high school classes with American children. They gave me a good impression. All of them were willing to speak in the class, but the Asians didn't speak a lot. They were brave to show their ideas.

I came to the US, so I can't rely on my parents anymore. I need to take care of myself and think about every decision and its consequences. I try to take care of my friends and others. I need to take care of myself. Finances problems will always be a big problem. What should I spend per month? What should I buy? I need to think about these problems every day. I try to reject buying some unnecessary items. Last week I saw some beautiful soccer shoes endorsed by Leo Messi. I wanted to buy them, but I thought about my finance problem, and I didn't buy them. The process of becoming independent makes me feel better. I feel I am growing up. In the future, I will be responsible in order to help my family. I want even more money to make my parent's life better.

ダイヤル市外通話

でんわ でん

市内通話もかけられます

A LANGUAGE LEARNER

Yanan Li

My life in the United States has changed me a lot, and adapting to my life here is mentally exhausting. In China, I was an employee at a company where I worked as a project manager. I was important to my group because I made the plans and told them what we should to do. I could also make some money for myself, so I didn't use money from my parents. I could afford things that I wanted. I didn't need to think too much about expenditures, except if I had enough to live on. In China, I had a lot of friends. We have known each other for many years and have common interests. In the United States, I am a language learner. I'm a student now, so that means I need to study all the time. It is difficult for me because my English is so poor. Therefore, I must spend a lot of time practicing, and I'm not able to do other things that I want to do. I feel tired every day. Because I don't have a job, I don't have financial resources. I have to pay for my tuition with my parent's money. I'm an adult now, so that makes me feel guilty and uncomfortable because paying adds to my parents' burden. I need to think about if I'm spending too much or if I really need these things. I have to find a way to reduce my expenses. In America, I want to make some new friends.

FROM TOTALLY SHY TO AN OUTGOING DANCER

Youjin Li

Before I come to the United States, I was a totally shy person. I was afraid to talk in front of many people and speak loudly outside. However, the life I spent in America changed me completely. In China, I used to learn new choreography online and practiced alone because I didn't want others look at me when I was dancing, even though I love dancing very much. After I came to the university, I joined a dancing club. My friends there encouraged me a lot. I realized that everyone could make a mistake and nobody would laugh at me. I even took part in a performance after I practiced for a month.

My club deeply changed my personality. Now I am much more outgoing than I was in China. I feel very appreciative for all of my friends who spent time with me in dancing club. Additionally, my communication skills also changed me from a person who was too shy to talk into a friendly, outgoing person. With my club member friends, I gradually got to know how Americans talk to each other. This is what I couldn't learn in China. Normally, English teachers in China only teach reading, writing, and listening skills. My speaking skills have improved a lot, not only from participating in class, but also from chatting with my American friends. In a word, I feel really appreciative for my new friends here. I am lucky that I came to Syracuse University because it changed me to a positive and outgoing person.

A SPECIAL AND DIFFICULT EXPERIENCE

Huan-Chen Tseng

Leaving my country Taiwan to study in the United States has been both a special and difficult experience. In Taiwan, I am the oldest grandson on both sides of my family, so I have more responsibilities and benefits than the other grandchildren. However, in the United States I'm just alone. The first month here was very difficult for me because I missed my family and friends a lot. I also thought about my family because I have some responsibilities that I can't do now. The second contrast is that in Taiwan I am an undergraduate college student with good friends in my college. I have a lot of friends in Taiwan. However, in the US, I am just an English Language Institute student. I am nobody in the United States because nobody knows me, and I don't have any friends here. Although there have been many difficult situations studying in the United States, I still think this is a special experience. I'm starting to make some new friends and starting to adapt to American habits. In the future, I will go back to Taiwan and finish my undergraduate degree. I think this experience will help me a lot in my future.

A GLOBAL VIEW

Chen Yang

I still remember the feeling of anxiety when I arrived at Syracuse Hancock airport for the first time. With so many questions and such curiosity, I started my new school life here. Time has passed quickly up to now. I have been in this new world for over one year and have gradually gotten used to the new environment. Now I am an independent and internationalized adult, instead of a dependent and narrow-minded child. I believe each international student must feel lonely at the beginning of their new life, having not made friends yet and being shocked by the new culture. Life in the United States has forced me to learn how to live without my parents. For example, I learned how to rent an apartment and take care of myself. I have faced a lot of difficulties for the first time, such as the language barrier, but I overcame them. I am becoming more independent. Furthermore, after becoming familiar with different cultures, I know more about the world. For example, I learned many Japanese women are willing to be a housewife, and many Arabian women cannot drive, despite being legally allowed to drive. It is interesting to see how people from other cultures give all of us a chance to learn by focusing on the essence and discard its dross. In brief, my view of the world has been widened. I was once a narrow-minded person, one who did not know that some people in the world are still suffering from hunger, poverty and war. I thought the world is peaceful and bright until I saw the darkness. In conclusion, life in America made me become independent and gave me a global view.

EXPECTATIONS OF LIVING IN AMERICA

Chuanjie Jian

I lived in China for nineteen years, and this was the first time I left my home for another country. There are numerous differences between living in China and living in America. Now, I have already stayed in Syracuse for six months. In this period, I have changed in many ways. I have changed my impression of America, developed my independent personality, and improved my study abilities.

First of all, my impression of America has changed. Before I came to the United States, I was very worried about an environment where Americans will have guns because I saw numerous news reports and TV shows where bad people use guns to commit a crime. For example, on 2016/6/12, I was watching television with my parents when the anchor said that there the biggest shooting happened in Orlando. A person used a gun to shoot many people, and finally caused forty-nine people to die. When I heard this news, I felt very unsafe. Therefore, I thought America is not safe. Moreover, some of my friends told me Americans do not like Chinese people. For instance, my best friend who has stayed in America for twelve years told me that when she did school projects with foreigners, the foreigners never wanted to talk with her and did not want to work with her. Thus, I was worried about this. Instead, now I have stayed in Syracuse for six months, my impression of America has changed. I feel very comfortable and excited. Americans are very kind. Not everyone has a gun, and Americans cannot use a gun in public places. Therefore, it is safer than I thought. In addition, now I think Americans are very helpful. When I have problems, they will be very happy to help me to solve problems. They told me they really like me and invited me to play with them. So, now, my impression of America has changed, and I feel America is a very good place.

Second, I have become more independent. When I lived in my home, I just needed to study and do whatever I wanted. I really relied on my parents in the same way that a princess really relies on her servants. I did not have to do the housework, such as clean the bedroom, wash clothes, and cook. My mom would do all of it for me. So, before I came to the United States, I was very worried about how to do these things by myself. However, now I have become more independent. I can tidy up the house. I can cook by myself. I can wash clothes. I have become more and more independent.

Finally, my study abilities have improved. When I lived in China, I did not have self-control. I devoted all my time to playing games and watching TV. If my mother supervised me, I would study hard. I always thought I studied hard because I wanted to make my parents be happy. On the contrary, when I came to the United States, nobody could supervise me to study. I needed to study by myself. In addition, I am impacted by my friends who study very hard in America. Now, I usually go to the library when I do not have class. Moreover, I think studying is for myself. The more knowledge I have, the more possible it is to get a job in the future. To sum up, while I have changed a lot in recent months, my change is still far behind my expectations. I really want to become better and better, in the same way that other successful international students have.

THE INTERNATIONAL STUDENTS

Xiangyi Wang

When the international students first go to the Syracuse, they are unfamiliar with everything around them. They have to do everything on their own. For example, the international students must take care of themselves. However, all international students can depend on their family to protect themselves, and they will become more familiar with their new hometown. I think they need a lot of time to adapt to the new environment and grow up by themselves. Under these circumstances, they also feel more depressed and sad than local students. It is the reason that people are tired in Syracuse. They will miss their family and hometown.

JACK AND ROSE
Jing Di

When Jack and Rose came to Syracuse, they were very confused on what they could do to adjust themselves, to adapt to their new environment. They were very perplexed in a small city, which isn't so famous that everyone knows about it. Jack and Rose didn't know much about Syracuse. Perplexed, helpless, and without assistance from their parents, they had to overcome problems by themselves. In conclusion, the life in Syracuse made Jack and Rose more confused and perplexed.

LIQUID REBECCA
Qiaochu Liu & Xiangjie Si

Her name is Rebecca. She is a liquid, which means she is able to be any shape she wants. She has a big brain, so she is much smarter than normal people. She has big ears, so she can hear a voice even if it comes from far away. For example, when she is attending biology class in a classroom, she can listen to the teacher who is giving another class in another classroom. Thus, she could learn two courses at the same time. Her heart is made of a lot of machine hands that can help her do several jobs. There is a super power in her eyes. She can control others by using her eyes, which can make people follow Rebecca's requirement. Also, she can see clearly at night. Therefore, she can do assignments in the dark, and she won't disrupt her roommate's sleep. She has everything in her pockets, including money, cars, and pets. She is a liquid. She won't get injured. Even if there are natural disasters, she can survive them. All in all, this is a perfect international student, Rebecca.

A BOY NAMED GENIUS

Zhengtong Xu

There is a boy who is named Genius, and he is so handsome. He has a big head, so he has a super-memory brain. He can remember everything that his professor taught, every bit of knowledge. Also, he can predict every exam's answer. He doesn't need to sleep, and he is never getting sick. He can write fast, so he can take notes very well when he listens to a lecture. He has a good comprehension, so he can understand everything from a lecture or class. Also, he can have a good chat with other classmates, so he has a good ability for making friends. In addition, he can create a lot of famous music, so he is musical genius. Remember him, his name is Genius.

Abraham

ABRAHAM THE EMPATHETIC

Bandar Alhoraibi

The video game character Abraham, who has a handsome appearance, has a lot of skills and super powers. His first ability is memorization. The reason why he can memorize everything is that he has a large brain that can hold a lot of information. His second super power is empathy. He can understand people's feelings and help them as much as possible because his ears can hear people's thoughts. His third ability is that he can never get sick because of his strong, healthy body. His fourth skill is controlling his emotions. To be more specific, he never feels sad or bad. He is the kind of person who is always happy and excited about doing anything. His fifth super power is the ability to teleport. For example, if Abraham needs to meet his professor immediately, he can arrive at the office in one second. His last ability is hating racism. This is because there is a lot of love in his heart. He can accept and respect everyone and everything that appears in the world. In short, Abraham is a perfect international student who has a lot of superpowers.

VERONICA WITH THE DARK HAIR

Anonymous

Once upon a time there was a girl named Veronica. She was a Chinese girl with long dark hair. She had big eyes with black cores. She has two big white wings, so she can fly wherever she wants. Her long dark hair stands for her being as beautiful and smart as an international student, which can help her make more friends. Her most obvious feature is that she has two ears like speakers, so she can hear anything, even sounds that are far away from her. Invisibility is one of her superpowers, too. She can be invisible around people and do whatever she wants. Okay, that's it.

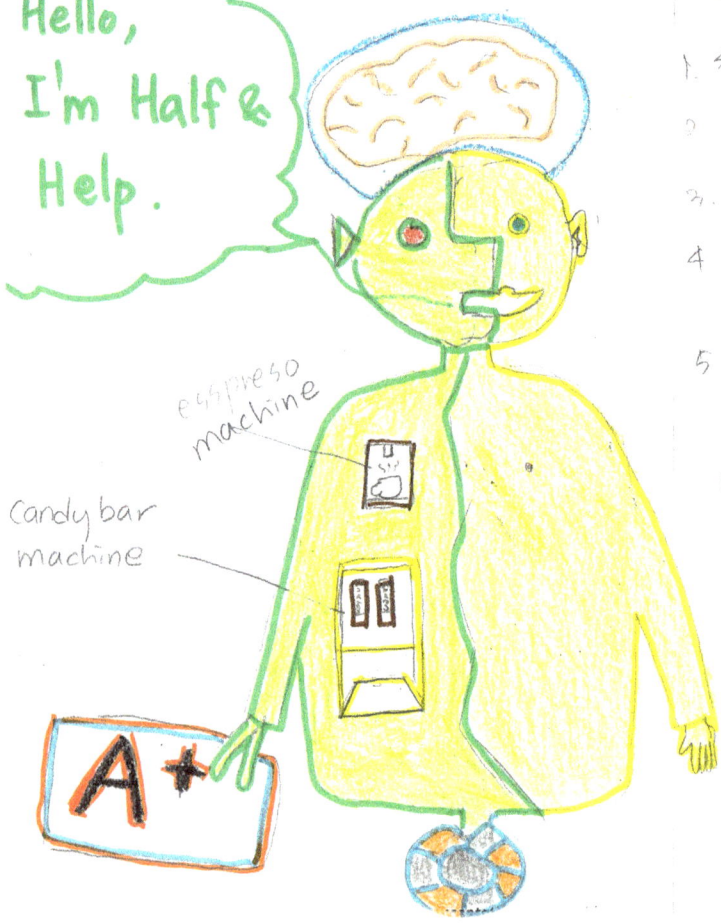

THE THREE BEST FUNCTIONS

Sun Ae Kim and Joakim Maaseidvaag Olsen

I am an international student who is always getting A's in class. I have a super head, which gives me the ability to remember everything. My eyes are on the right side, which is my mechanical side. They help to record and store information. I never forget everything. The candy bar machine on my mechanical side helps students get energy. Besides the candy bar machine, I have an espresso machine for everyone to use. It gives students the ability to stay awake for classes. Lastly, I have a wheel which helps me travel back and forth easily and without any cost. To sum up, having a fantastic head, the ability to help other students focus on classes, and a wheel that allows me to travel without costs are the three best functions for earning an A in every class.

A RECORD OF MY FAMILY

Wenkai Zhuang

I think "home" means the whole family and the whole clan. There is a record that includes all of my family members' information since the 1750's. It is from first generation to twenty-fifth generation. I am in the twenty-fifth generation. The record is really meaningful and interesting. There is one interesting part that our clan immigrated from northern China to southern China.

Some significant, remarkable, and traditional rituals have been preserved from a long time ago. During Spring Festival, all my family members stay together and take part in the traditional ritual. In this ritual, one of the oldest or whoever is in a high position in family, leads the whole family to remember our ancestors. It is really important because we should not forget our family's route, the place we lived, or our family story. It is enjoyable that the whole family (twenty to thirty people) stays together. Males can discuss political issues and the market. Women can talk about some daily event in their small family. Each year, we only have one time that our family can stay together. We can see some changes in our family members, like who becomes fat or who has a baby. It is relaxing.

RE/VISING HOME:
The Gift of International Student Perspectives
Charissa Che

"Stories can provide us with a sense of belonging, can appeal to our desire to belong, or even confirm our belief that we do not quite fit in."
— Morris Young, *Minor Re/Visions: Asian American Literacy Narratives as a Rhetoric of Citizenship* (2004)

In *Minor Re/visions*, Morris Young proposes that minority students engage in a process of "minor re/vision"; that is, a rhetorical means by which they can interact with and respond to a dominant culture, in their own words and on their own terms (29). He begins his book by enacting a "personal re/vision" of his own: first, he recounts a visit to his primary school's speech therapist – a hazy memory tinted by feelings of confusion, anxiety, and exclusion. Then comes an aside: "As I reflect back on my life it is not surprising that some of my most vivid memories from my childhood are about language…I wonder how much this early experience with language has shaped my life" (18-20). I am reminded of Young's memory as I read the brief yet potent student testimonies by students in the English Language Institute at Syracuse University.

In my view, the forty-one international students in this collection have gifted us with stories that are "re/visions" in their own right. They are at times painful to read; at others, triumphant. In having left their home countries to study English at Syracuse University, these students give readers, namely those who have not studied abroad or faced the task of adapting to a new culture and language, a nuanced perspective on the "U.S. university experience."

But before going further on why this book matters, I beg a central question, and a few follow-ups: *What is "home"?* Consequently: what does it mean to *leave* home; *miss* home?

While perhaps trite, the American idiom, *Home is where the heart is,* may be a good start to answering the first question. In fact, Chinese international student Ai Guan cites it at the beginning of her narrative, "Home Always Waits for Me," before professing that her heart resides with her family, the feelings of warmth and safety they bring her, and the Chinese holidays they've celebrated together. Similarly, in "In My Home," Yuan Cheng's nostalgia came from remembering the plants in her family's garden, playing with her siblings, and the distinct smell of her mother. In "Lovely Summer," Haochen Feng recalls "one of the best summers" of her life, filled with visits to hot springs and the movies in Northern China with her boyfriend and his family.

Haochen's piece prompts me to ponder what it means to *leave* home. Many of us have probably felt a similar bittersweetness between our own high school graduation and heading off to college, but likely fewer of us have faced leaving our home country for a new one, to learn a second language and a second culture, all while tackling a new learning environment. Yet, we can empathize with her, as well as with the anonymous writer of "Speak Well and Make Friends" who tells us her "mind was very complex" during her plane ride from China to America. Leaving can also be a catalyst for rebirth: Chuanjie Jian reminds us in "Expectations of Living in America" that an introduction to new people and places can expand our worldview and fundamentally change us for the better. And as for what it means to *miss* home? For Chuanjie, it was the anxiety of leaving her parents to take care of themselves. Unlike "local" (domestic) students, Xiangyi Wang thinks he and his fellow international student peers feel a deeper sense of withdrawal from home because the protection offered to them by their parents is unreachable: "It is the reason that people are tired in Syracuse," she writes in "The International Students."

In exploring the notion of "home," the authors in this collection achieve "re/visions" that tie the personal to the social. They evoke familiar themes of homesickness, childhood memories, and the exciting yet daunting prospect of change. Additionally, they inform and connect us, *because*, not *in spite,* of the unfamiliarity in their experiences from our own. And where there *are* disparities, they have created sites for cross-cultural learning, compassion, and acknowledgment of our own privileges. Their writing demonstrates that minority students finding themselves in the contact zone of their "home" and new "host" cultures can wield their stories to cope with change and negotiate their self-identities in generative, community-building ways.

What's more, publishing these students' work in New City Community Press can push international students' voices and identities to the fore of teachers', university administrators', and curricula designers' attentions. Given that the majority of the students featured are from China, we have an even greater obligation to acknowledge the value of this work in challenging the stereotype historically attributed to "Chinese learners" as passive and uncritical, possessing a homogenous set of values, personality traits, and learning styles (Clark and Gieve 54-55). The stories in this collection cogently debunk these perceptions by positioning international students as agents in their own thinking.

If our writing instructors use this book as a model for praxis, the next steps could be exciting. Consider the possibilities of deliberately mobilizing student stories in the classroom by inviting students to respond to each other's work, and reflect on their experiences alongside the work of more "established" scholars on their syllabi. Min-Zhan Lu writes in "Professing Multiculturalism: The Politics of Style in the Contact Zone" that "such reading and revision of their own writing allows students to enter into dialogue with 'real' writers as 'fellow travelers,' active learners eager to compare and contrast one another's trials and triumphs" (457). Instead of feeling intimidated by them, students learn to see other scholars as *storytellers* and real *people* much like themselves: individuals they could trust, converse with, and even challenge.

Whether read as standalone pieces or in conjunction with others' work, we have much to learn from these students' testimonies. The international students in this book capture the essence of the above epigraph from Young to a tee: their stories can indeed give us a feeling of belongingness in a community, assure us that we are not alone in wanting to belong, or affirm our anxieties that we don't belong, after all. The transitionary moment of leaving home for college can be fraught no matter a student's background, and knowing this can paradoxically provide solace for college students seeking a "home" away from home, wherever or whatever their home is.

I realize that after all this (and despite using "home" profusely in my last sentence), I still haven't provided concrete answers for my questions on what "home" is – what it means to leave it, and miss it. This omission is deliberate and incidental. Deliberate, because our sense of "home" will no doubt change constantly over the course of our lives. As a Chinese American, I looked back on the acculturative obstacles I'd faced in simply moving across the country for school, and found my sense of "home" disrupted with each student narrative I read. The omission is incidental, in that I was in Salt Lake City, Utah, when I read these students' words, and

I am sitting in a library in New York City as I write this afterword.

I think now of the foods, traditions, and stories I was raised on, in a new light. How serendipitous it is, that I came home for the first time in nearly a year to write about home. And how fortunate it is, that we have stories to teach us about ourselves and each other as we continue to traverse uncharted territories.

Works Cited

Clark, Rose, and Simon N. Gieve. "On the Discursive Construction of 'the Chinese Learner'." *Language, Culture and Curriculum*, vol. 19, no. 1, 2006, pp. 54--73.

Lu, Min-Zhan. "Professing Multiculturalism: The Politics of Style in the Contact Zone." *College Composition and Communication*, vol. 45, no. 4, 1994, pp. 442–58.

Young, Morris. *Minor Re/Visions: Asian American Literacy Narratives as a Rhetoric of Citizenship*. Southern Illinois UP, 2004.

Note on the Manuscript

In editing this manuscript, every effort was made to retain the voices of the authors, many of whom were writing in a second language new to them. Changes were made to the sentence structure only when specific words and colloquial phrases were clearly misused or misspelled. Each piece was also edited to eliminate phrasings related to specific assignments or contexts unrelated to the topic of the piece. When a piece had dual authorship, only the author who wished to have their name included in the manuscript was cited. Finally, each author provided with at least two opportunities to review and revise their text prior to publication.

www.ingramcontent.com/pod-product-compliance
Lightning Source LLC
Chambersburg PA
CBHW051439270326
41931CB00020B/3483